# HOMEMADE HEALTH

Spoil Your Furry Friend With Mouthwatering, Nourishing, And Easy-To-Make Recipes That Will Make Their Tail Wag With Joy!

Complete Guide To Feed Your Furry Friend Safely Included

**JASMINE FOSTER**

Copyright © 2024 by Jasmine Foster

All content within this book and any accompanying materials, is protected by copyright. No part of this publication may be reproduced, distributed, or transmitted in any form or by any means, including photocopying, recording, or other electronic or mechanical methods, without the prior written permission of the publisher, except in the case of brief quotations embodied in critical reviews and certain other noncommercial uses permitted by copyright law. For permission requests, please contact the publisher.

Medical Disclaimer

This cookbook for dogs provides recipes intended for canine consumption only. Consult with a veterinarian before making any dietary changes or if your dog has specific health concerns. The information in this cookbook is not a substitute for professional veterinary advice, diagnosis, or treatment. Always prioritize your dog's well-being and consult a veterinarian for tailored dietary guidance.

Could you kindly leave a review on Amazon if you like the book and find it helpful? It only takes a few seconds, but it's very important to me. You can do it by scanning the following QR code with your phone. Thank you.

# INTRODUCTION ... 7
## Canned Or Home-Made Ready-Made Food? ... 8
## The 5 Tips About Making Homemade Dog Food ... 12
## The Different Nutrients Your Dog Needs ... 13

# THE BASICS OF DOG NUTRITION ... 17
## The 12 Laws You Must Follow If You Care About Your Dog ... 20
## Foods To Absolutely Avoid ... 21
## How To Tell If Your Dog Has The Right Weight ... 24
## Food Allergies, How To Deal With Them ... 25
## Monitoring Your Dog's Health And Preventing Common Health Issues ... 27
## Avoiding The Most Frequent Health Problems ... 28

# FEW RULES BEFOR STARTING ... 30

# MEAT ... 33
Zucchini and Chicken Bites ... 34
Ground Beef and Sweet Potato ... 35
Turkey and Vegetable Stew ... 35
Lamb and Lentil Soup ... 37
Beef Meatballs ... 38
Chicken and Liver Pâté ... 39
Turkey and Cranberry Stuffing ... 40
Ground Beef and Pumpkin Chili ... 41
Chicken and Vegetable Soup ... 42
Beef Stew ... 43
Chicken Pot Pie ... 44
Pork and Apple Sauce ... 45
Chicken and Rice ... 46
Zucchini and Chicken Bites ... 46
Chicken and Green Bean Soup ... 47
Turkey and Sweet Potato Mash ... 48
Chicken and Quinoa ... 49

Lamb and Lentils ............................................................................. 49
Turkey and Sweet Potato Mash ...................................................... 50

## FISH ............................................................................................. 51

Fish and Sweet Potato .................................................................... 52
Salmon and Oatmeal Pancakes ...................................................... 52
Salmon and Quinoa ........................................................................ 53
Salmon and Peas ............................................................................ 54
Tuna and Rice ................................................................................. 54
Salmon and Oatmeal ...................................................................... 55
Sardines and Yogurt ....................................................................... 55
Fish and Potato ............................................................................... 56
Frozen Fish and Carrot Pops .......................................................... 57
Fish and Apple Mash ...................................................................... 57
Sardines and Blueberries ............................................................... 58
Fish and Vegetable Soup ................................................................ 58
Fish and Oat Muffins ...................................................................... 59
Fish and Peanut Butter Frosty Paws .............................................. 60
Tuna and Spinach Treats ................................................................ 61

## VEGETABLES ................................................................................. 62

Sweet Potato and Carrot Mash ....................................................... 63
Pumpkin Pupsicles .......................................................................... 63
Pumpkin and Oatmeal Muffins ....................................................... 64
Sweet Potato Chews ....................................................................... 65
Carrot Crunchies ............................................................................. 66
Pumpkin Dog Biscuits ..................................................................... 66
Broccoli Muffins .............................................................................. 67
Apple and Carrot Crunchers .......................................................... 68

## EXTRA ........................................................................................... 69

Peanut Butter and Banana ............................................................. 70
Pumpkin and Peanut Butter Ice Cream ......................................... 70
Green Bean Smoothie ..................................................................... 71
Pumpkin and Peanut Butter Ice Cream ......................................... 72
Peanut Butter and Banana Dog Cookies ....................................... 72

Fruit pudding ............................................................................. 73
Carrot Muffins ........................................................................... 74
Hard-Boiled Egg and Oatmeal ................................................ 75
Scrambled Egg and Toast ....................................................... 75
Peanut Butter Kong .................................................................. 76
Frozen Banana Pops ................................................................ 76
Apple Muffins ............................................................................. 77
Zucchini and Peanut Butter Cookies ..................................... 78
Peanut Butter Frosting ............................................................. 79
Peanut Butter Banana Bites ................................................... 79
Apple Slices ............................................................................... 80
Banana Popsicles ..................................................................... 80
Zucchini Bites ............................................................................ 81
Banana Oat Biscuits ................................................................. 81

## CONCLUSION ............................................................... 83

## 7 MISTAKES YOU MIGHT BE MAKING WITH YOUR DOG'S NUTRITION ...................................................................... 88

## UNLEASHING THE MAGIC OF DOG TRAINING .................. 93

## LET'S HAVE FUN TOGETHER! ........................................... 98

# INTRODUCTION

The Homemade nutritious Dog Food Cookbook & Blueprint is a step-by-step guide to providing a nutritious and balanced food to your dog, whether you're a novice or a seasoned pro. This book is for anybody who wishes to feed their dog nutritious and tasty food. This book contains something for everyone, whether you're a novice dog owner or have been feeding your dog for years.

The book is broken into two parts:

## BOOK 1: THE FUNDAMENTALS OF DOG NUTRITION

This section of the book covers the fundamentals of canine nutrition, such as the many nutrients your dog need, how much food to give your dog, and how to calculate your dog's calorie requirements. You'll learn about the significance of protein, carbs, fats, vitamins, and minerals in your dog's diet, as well as how to make sure your dog gets enough of them. You'll also discover how to determine your dog's calorie requirements depending on their age, breed, activity level, and overall health.

BOOK 2: EASY AND QUICK RECIPES

This section of the book provides 100 homemade dog food recipes. All of the recipes use simple, easy-to-find ingredients and are quick and straightforward to create. The recipes are divided into categories to facilitate searching.

By the conclusion of this book, you'll know everything you need to know about feeding a nutritious and balanced diet to your dog. You'll also gain access to a library of 100 tasty and nutritious recipes.

## Canned Or Home-Made Ready-Made Food?

### Why feed your dog homemade food?

Making your own dog food is a terrific method to guarantee that your dog is getting a balanced and nutritious diet. When you create your own food, you have total control over the ingredients, ensuring that your dog gets what he or she requires without the use of unneeded additives or fillers.

One of the primary benefits of feeding your dog homemade food is the flexibility to tailor the diet to your four-legged friend's individual requirements. You may select the best, highest-quality components while eliminating the low-quality ingredients that are commonly found in commercial dog food. To supply your dog with high-quality protein, vitamins, and fiber, choose lean, high-quality meat, fresh veggies, and whole grains.

You may also customize your dog's food to any allergies or intolerances they may have. If your dog has certain nutritional demands, you may readily modify recipes to satisfy those needs. This degree of management is especially critical if your dog has health difficulties or dietary restrictions.

It is crucial to realize that feeding your dog homemade food does not need you to prepare every meal from scratch. Many quick and easy recipes are available online or in dog food cookbooks, allowing you to create nutritious meals without spending too much time in the kitchen. You may also plan ahead of time and create larger servings, storing leftovers for future meals. This is especially useful for folks who lead hectic lifestyles yet want to ensure their dog eats healthily.

In conclusion, giving your dog homemade food is a wonderful way to guarantee that your pet is getting a high-quality diet that is suited to their unique needs. It's a kind approach to provide properly prepared, fresh, and nutritious food for your dog's well-being.

## Benefits of Homemade Dog Food

There are good reasons for preferring home-made food to store-bought products, which are often poor and expensive, let's see them

1. A healthier coat and skin: Homemade dog food is often made with fresh, whole ingredients that are packed with nutrients that support a healthy coat and skin. For example, omega-3 fatty acids, found in fish oil and flaxseed oil, can help to reduce inflammation and itching, while vitamin A can help to promote healthy cell growth and repair.

2. Stronger immune system: Homemade dog food can help to boost your dog's immune system by providing them with a variety of essential vitamins and minerals. For example, vitamin C helps to produce white blood cells, which fight infection, while vitamin E is a powerful antioxidant that protects cells from damage.

3. Improved digestion: Homemade dog food is often easier for dogs to digest than commercial food, which can lead to less gas and bloating. This is because homemade food is typically made with fewer processed ingredients and more fresh, whole foods. For example, cooked brown rice is a good source of fiber, which can help to keep the digestive system healthy.

4. Reduced risk of chronic diseases: Homemade dog food can help to reduce your dog's risk of developing chronic diseases such as obesity, diabetes, and arthritis. This is because homemade food is typically lower in calories and unhealthy fats than commercial food. Additionally, homemade food can be tailored to your dog's individual needs, such as if they have any allergies or sensitivities.

5. More energy: Homemade dog food can give your dog more energy so they can enjoy their favorite activities. This is because homemade food is typically made with more nutritious ingredients than commercial food. For example, lean protein, such as chicken or fish, can provide your dog with a sustained source of energy.

6. Better appetite: Homemade food is often more palatable to dogs than commercial food, which can lead to a better appetite. This is because homemade food is typically made with more flavorful ingredients and less processed fillers. For example, adding a small amount of cooked pumpkin to your dog's food can help to make it more appealing.

7. Stronger bond with you: Cooking for your dog is a great way to show them how much you love them. It's also a fun and rewarding experience that can help to strengthen your bond. Additionally, cooking for your dog allows you to control the ingredients in their food and ensure that they are getting a healthy and balanced diet.

Let's see what it takes to produce a wholesome food besides our love...

# The 5 Tips About Making Homemade Dog Food

It's easy to make food for our beloved dogs, but there are a few things you need to know to do a good job.

Here are 5 tips about making homemade dog food:

1. Do your homework: Before you begin creating homemade dog food, do your homework and speak with a veterinarian to verify that you are giving a healthy diet for your dog. There are several resources available online and in libraries to assist you in getting started.
2. Use premium ingredients: It is critical to utilize high-quality items when cooking for your dog. Avoid processed meals, fizzy drinks, and trans fats. Instead, use fresh, complete products that are high in nutrition.
3. Be mindful of portion sizes: It is critical to give your dog the proper portion amount. Overfeeding can lead to obesity, which can cause a variety of health issues. You can check with your veterinarian or use a feeding calculator to establish the proper meal size for your dog.
4. Mix and match: It is critical to provide your dog with a range of diets to ensure that they are getting all of the nutrients they require. Experiment with different recipes and ingredients to see what your dog prefers. You may also

season your dog's meal with other ingredients such as yogurt, pumpkin, or sweet potato.
5. Properly store leftovers: If you have leftovers, make sure to carefully store them. Homemade dog food may be refrigerated for up to three days or frozen for up to three months. When reheating leftover food, make sure it is properly cooked through before serving.

Here's an extra tip:

6. Have fun! Cooking with your dog may be a rewarding and enjoyable experience. Try new stuff and be creative with your cooking. You might be surprised at what your dog likes to eat.

# The Different Nutrients Your Dog Needs

Dogs need a variety of nutrients to stay healthy, including:

**Protein**

Protein is essential for dogs of all ages, but it is especially important for puppies and senior dogs. Puppies need protein to grow and develop, while senior dogs need protein to maintain their muscle mass. Good sources of protein for dogs include meat, poultry, fish, eggs, and dairy products.

## Carbohydrates

Carbohydrates provide dogs with energy. Good sources of carbohydrates for dogs include whole grains, such as brown rice and oats, as well as fruits and vegetables.

## Fat

Fat is an important nutrient for dogs, but it is important to feed them the right type of fat. Saturated and unhealthy fats can lead to weight gain and other health problems. Instead, focus on feeding your dog healthy fats, such as those found in fish oil, flaxseed oil, and animal fats.

## Vitamins and minerals

Vitamins and minerals are essential for a variety of bodily functions, including immune system function, digestion, and bone health. Good sources of vitamins and minerals for dogs include fruits, vegetables, and fortified dog food.

**Carbohydrates**

Carbohydrates provide dogs with energy, but they should be fed in moderation. Too many carbohydrates can lead to weight gain and other health problems. Good sources of carbohydrates for dogs include whole grains, such as brown rice and oats, as well as fruits and vegetables.

**Calories**

The number of calories a dog needs depends on a number of factors, including their age, breed, activity level, and body condition. A general rule of thumb is to feed a dog between 25 and 30 calories per pound of body weight per day. However, it is important to talk to your veterinarian to determine the best feeding plan for your individual dog.

## How to distribute these macronutrients

The following is a general guideline for how to distribute the macronutrients in your dog's diet:

- ✓ Protein: 25-30%
- ✓ Fat: 10-15%

- ✓ Carbohydrates: 55-65%

It is important to note that these are just general guidelines. The best way to determine the ideal macronutrient distribution for your dog is to talk to your veterinarian.

Following these guidelines can assist you in making nutritious and delicious homemade dog food that your dog will like.

# THE BASICS OF DOG NUTRITION

Almost every dog owner overfeeds their pet. This is due to the difficulty of resisting those large, begging eyes! Overfeeding, on the other hand, can lead to major health issues like as obesity, diabetes, and arthritis.

The amount of food you should give your dog is determined by several factors, including their breed, age, activity level, and bodily condition. Of course, varied dog breeds have varied nutritional requirements. Toy breeds, for example, require less food than huge animals. Puppies require more food than adult dogs, while older dogs may require less. Sedentary dogs require less food than active canines.

It is critical to consult with your veterinarian to identify the appropriate feeding plan for your specific dog. However, the following are some general guidelines:

- 1/4 cup to 1 cup of food each day for toy breeds
- 1 cup to 1 2/5 cup of food each day for small breeds
- 2 cups to 2 2/3 cups of food each day for medium breeds
- Large breeds require 2 1/2 to 3 cups of food every day.

It is also critical to provide your dog with high-quality food. Look for a meal that is suitable for your dog's age, breed, and level of exercise. Avoid meals with a lot of fillers and artificial additives.

# How to calculate your dog's calorie needs

You will need to know your dog's weight, age, activity level, and bodily condition to determine their calorie needs.

Weight: The first step is for your dog to be weighed. This may be done at home or at the office of your veterinarian.

Age: The age of your dog will also influence their calorie requirements. Puppies require more calories than adult dogs, however elderly dogs may require fewer calories than adult dogs.

Level of Activity: Your dog's exercise level will also influence their calorie requirements. Sedentary dogs require less calories than active dogs.

Physical condition: Your dog's bodily condition will also influence their calorie requirements. If your dog is overweight or obese, he or she will require less calories than a dog of normal weight.

Once you've gathered this information, you may use a calorie calculator to calculate your dog's daily calorie requirements. There are several calorie calculators accessible online, but you can also seek advice from your veterinarian.

The daily calorie requirements of a dog can be calculated using the National Research Council (NRC) energy maintenance formula for dogs:

Daily Calorie Requirement (in kcal) = $(30 * \text{Weight in kg}) + (70 * \text{Weight in kg})^{3/4}$

where:

**Weight in kg** is the weight of the dog in kilograms.

30 represents an approximate estimate of the **basal calorie** requirement of an inactive dog (also known as basal metabolism).

70 represents an approximate value used to estimate the additional calorie requirement due to **physical activity**.

Please note that this is only an approximate calculation, and the actual calorie requirement of the dog may vary based on factors such as age, breed, activity level, and health status. Therefore, it is important to consult a veterinarian to obtain a more accurate estimate of your dog's daily calorie needs.

Here's a practical example of calculating the daily calorie requirement for a dog:

Let's say we have a dog weighing 15 kilograms (kg) with a moderate level of physical activity. Using the NRC formula:

Daily Calorie Requirement (in kcal) = (30 * Weight in kg) + (70 * Weight in kg)^(3/4)

Daily Calorie Requirement = (30 * 15 kg) + (70 * 15 kg)^(3/4)

Daily Calorie Requirement = (450) + (70 * 3.87298) [Calculating the cube root]

Daily Calorie Requirement = 450 + 271.0966

The approximate daily calorie requirement for this 15 kg dog with a moderate activity level would be around 721 kilocalories (kcal) per day.

# The 12 Laws You Must Follow If You Care About Your Dog

**Rule 1:** Dogs' dietary requirements vary depending on their life stage. Puppies, for example, have higher calorie and nutritional requirements than adult dogs. Nutritional requirements are also influenced by breed. Working dogs, for example, require more calories and nutrients than other breeds. The degree of activity also influences dietary requirements. Sedentary dogs require less calories and nutrients than active canines.

**Rule 2:** Obesity may be caused by overfeeding, which increases the risk of a variety of health problems such as heart disease, diabetes, and arthritis.

**Rule 3:** A variety of diets can assist ensure that your dog gets all of the nutrients he or she requires.

**Rule 4:** Processed meals are frequently heavy in calories, bad fats, and salt. They may also include harmful artificial chemicals, preservatives, and colorings. Sugary beverages like soda and juice can cause weight gain, dental damage, and other health issues. Trans fats and saturated fats, for example, can raise the risk of heart disease, stroke, and other health concerns.

**Rule 5:** Regular feeding times might help your dog stay healthy and avoid overeating.

**Rule 6:** Water that is fresh and pure is crucial for hydration and general wellness.

**Rule 7:** Your veterinarian is the most knowledgeable about your dog's nutritional requirements.

**Rule 8:** Table scraps contain a lot of calories and bad fats. They can also result in begging and other behavioral issues.

**Rule 9:** Chocolate, grapes, and onions, among other human delicacies, can be poisonous to dogs.

**Rule 10:** Raw food diets can be deadly if not properly prepared. Bacteria that can make your dog sick can be found in raw meat.

**Rule 11:** Home-cooked foods might be challenging to balance and suit your dog's nutritional demands. It is critical to collaborate with a veterinarian or veterinary nutritionist to develop a safe and healthful diet.

**Rule 12:** Changing diets abruptly might cause stomach distress. It is critical to gently introduce a new diet to your dog.

## Foods To Absolutely Avoid

Let us now see which foods are harmful to our furry friends:

- **Chocolate**: Chocolate contains theobromine, which is toxic to dogs. The amount of theobromine that is toxic to a dog varies depending on the type of chocolate and the size of the dog. Dogs who eat chocolate may experience symptoms such as vomiting, diarrhea, restlessness, tremors, and seizures. In severe cases, chocolate can even be fatal.

- **Grapes and raisins**: Grapes and raisins can cause kidney failure in dogs. Symptoms of kidney failure include vomiting, diarrhea, lethargy, and loss of appetite. In severe cases, kidney failure can be fatal.
- **Avocado**: Avocado contains persin, which is toxic to dogs. Symptoms of avocado poisoning include vomiting, diarrhea, and respiratory problems.
- **Onions and garlic**: Onions and garlic can cause anemia in dogs. Symptoms of anemia include lethargy, lack of appetite, and weakness.
- **Macadamia** nuts: Macadamia nuts can cause tremors, lethargy, vomiting, and diarrhea in dogs.
- **Chicken and turkey bones**: Chicken and turkey bones can splinter and cause internal injuries to dogs.
- **Alcohol**: Alcohol is toxic to dogs. Symptoms of alcohol poisoning include vomiting, diarrhea, lethargy, and seizures.
- **Caffeine**: Caffeine is toxic to dogs. Symptoms of caffeine poisoning include vomiting, diarrhea, tremors, and seizures.
- **Xylitol**: Xylitol is an artificial sweetener that is toxic to dogs. Xylitol can cause a rapid drop in blood sugar levels, which can lead to seizures, coma, and even death.
- **Sweets**: Sweets are often high in calories, fat, and sugar, which can lead to obesity and other health problems in dogs.
- **Raw meat**: Raw meat can contain bacteria that can cause illness in dogs.

- **Milk and dairy** products: Many dogs are lactose intolerant. Consuming milk or dairy products can cause diarrhea and other digestive problems.

Other products to avoid include these:

- **Fatty foods:** Fatty foods can cause pancreatitis in dogs, a serious inflammation of the pancreas. Pancreatitis can be fatal if left untreated.

- **Foods high in saturated and trans fats:** Saturated and trans fats are unhealthy for dogs and can increase the risk of heart disease, stroke, and other health problems.

- **Fried foods:** Fried foods are high in fat and calories and can contribute to obesity, which can lead to a number of health problems, including heart disease, diabetes, and arthritis.

- **Foods cooked with strong spices or condiments:** Strong spices and condiments can irritate the dog's stomach and intestines. This can lead to vomiting, diarrhea, and other digestive problems.

- **Spoiled or contaminated foods:** Spoiled or contaminated foods can contain harmful bacteria that can cause food poisoning in dogs. Food poisoning can cause vomiting, diarrhea, fever, and other symptoms.

It is important to remember that even small amounts of some of these foods can be harmful to dogs. If your dog eats any of these foods, it is important to contact your veterinarian immediately.

## How To Tell If Your Dog Has The Right Weight

You may check your dog's body condition score (BCS) to see whether they are the proper weight. A dog's body fat percentage is evaluated using the BCS, a 9-point scale. An optimal score is 4 or 5, whereas a score of 3 or below indicates underweight, while a score of 6 or above indicates overweight.

You may observe your dog's physique from above and from the side to determine their BCS. Your dog should have an hourglass form when viewed from above, with their waist tucked in behind their ribs. You should be able to perceive a small tuck in their belly while looking at them from the side. Additionally, you should be able to feel their ribs without exerting much pressure.

Ask your veterinarian for advice if you're unsure of your dog's BCS. If necessary, they can also provide you suggestions on how to assist your dog in gaining or losing weight.

Here are some more guidelines for determining your dog's ideal weight:

Feel their ribs, please. Without exerting much pressure, you ought to be able to feel the ribs of your dog. Your dog is certainly overweight if you can't feel their ribs. Your dog probably needs to gain weight if you can readily see their ribs.

Observe their waistline. Your dog should have an hourglass form when viewed from above, with their waist tucked in behind their ribs. If there is no waistline visible, your dog probably weighs too much.

Look at their belly. You ought should be able to perceive a little tuck in their abdomen when seen from the side. Your dog is probably overweight if their abdomen sags.

## Food Allergies, How To Deal With Them

Dog food allergies are a prevalent cause of skin, intestinal, and other health problems in dogs. Food allergies develop when a dog's immune system reacts abnormally to a certain food or substance.

Proteins from chicken, beef, dairy, eggs, and wheat are the most prevalent dietary allergies in dogs. Soy, maize, and pork are other possible allergies.

Food allergies in dogs can cause a variety of symptoms, depending on the dog and the degree of the allergy. Among the most prevalent symptoms are:

- Dry skin
- Skin redness and inflammation
- Hives
- Paw and foot licking and chewing
- Diarrhea and vomiting
- Loss of weight

It is essential to consult a veterinarian if you feel your dog has a food allergy. They can do tests to establish whether your dog has a food allergy and assist you in developing a safe and healthy diet for your dog.

**Food allergy management in dogs**

Avoiding the allergen is the best strategy to control food allergies in dogs. Once the allergy has been discovered, your veterinarian can assist you in developing a healthy diet for your dog. This diet might be a commercial or homemade hypoallergenic diet.

If your dog is on a homemade diet, it is critical that it be full and balanced. You can construct a homemade diet for your dog in collaboration with a veterinarian or veterinary nutritionist.

There are a few additional things you can do to help your dog with food allergies:

- Regularly bathe your dog to help eliminate allergies from their skin and coat.
- Utilize hypoallergenic shampoo and conditioner to lessen the risk of irritation.
- Do not feed your dog table leftovers. Table crumbs may include allergens that will cause an allergy to flare up.

# Monitoring Your Dog's Health And Preventing Common Health Issues

Being alert and knowing what is usual for your dog is the greatest method to monitor his or her health. This involves observing your dog's behavior, physical health, weight, and feeding habits.

**Behavior**: Behavior changes, such as tiredness, decreased appetite, or increased thirst, might indicate a health condition. For example, if your dog is generally energetic and lively but becomes sluggish suddenly, this might be an indication of disease.

**Physical condition**: Without pressing too firmly, you should be able to feel your dog's ribs. If you can't feel your dog's ribs, he's probably overweight. If you can plainly see your dog's ribs, he is probably underweight. When seen from the side, you should be able to discern a little tuck in your dog's tummy. If your dog's belly sags, he is most likely overweight.

**Weight**: Weighing your dog on a regular basis allows you to keep track of their health and discover any possible concerns. Weight increase or decrease might indicate a health issue. For example, if your dog gains a lot of weight all of a sudden, it might be an indication of a thyroid condition.

**Dietary habits**: Changes in eating patterns, such as reduced or increased appetite, might potentially indicate a health issue. For example, if your dog generally eats two meals a day but suddenly starts eating only one, this might indicate sickness.

In addition to the foregoing, you should keep an eye on your dog's feces and urine. Any changes in stool or urine, such as diarrhea, vomiting, or blood in the urine, may indicate a medical concern.

It is critical to consult your veterinarian if you observe any changes in your dog's behavior, bodily condition, weight, feeding habits, feces, or urine. It is critical to diagnose and address health concerns in your dog as soon as possible.

## Avoiding The Most Frequent Health Problems

There are several things you can do to help prevent some of the most frequent health problems in dogs. These are some examples:

**Providing a high-quality diet** for your dog. A balanced food can assist your dog in maintaining a healthy weight and immune system. Look for a comprehensive and balanced dog food that is suited for your dog's age, breed, and activity level when selecting a food.

**Provide frequent exercise for your dog**. Exercise is essential for keeping a healthy weight and lowering the chance of acquiring health conditions such as arthritis and heart disease. Aim for at least 30 minutes of exercise every day for your dog.

**Regularly grooming your dog** Grooming is essential for keeping your dog's skin and coat healthy and parasite-free. Brush your dog's teeth at least three times a week and bathe them once a month.

**Socialization of your dog**. A well-socialized dog is less prone to develop behavioral issues that might lead to health issues. From an early age, socialize your dog by introducing them to a range of people, places, and circumstances.

Aside from the aforementioned, there are a few particular things you can do to assist prevent common health concerns in dogs. These are some examples:

Obesity Prevention: Obesity is a serious health issue in dogs. It can cause various health issues including arthritis, diabetes, and heart disease. Feed your dog a balanced food and exercise them on a regular basis to prevent obesity.

Dental disease prevention: Another major health issue in dogs is dental problems. It can cause discomfort, tooth loss, and infection. Brush your dog's teeth at least three times a week to prevent dental problems, and take them to the veterinarian for dental cleanings when needed.

Parasite prevention: Fleas, ticks, and heartworms can all cause a range of health issues in dogs. Use a parasite preventive product advised by your veterinarian to avoid parasites.

Infection prevention: Infections that dogs can catch include parvovirus, distemper, and kennel cough. Vaccinate your dog according to your veterinarian's advice to prevent them from infection.

You can assist to monitor your dog's health and prevent the most frequent health disorders by following these guidelines.

The second section of the book is a collection of recipes that I have accumulated over the years while working with dogs. As a result, they have been thoroughly tested and universally accepted! They are easy dishes with few ingredients that are also healthful and nutritious. They contain no preservatives or colorings and may be produced fast.

Tip: Get creative with your recipes! There are endless possibilities when it comes to homemade dog food. You can use a variety of ingredients to create meals that are both healthy and delicious for your dog. So have fun and experiment!

## FEW RULES BEFOR STARTING

Before you start preparing these succulent dishes, consider the following general rules, some we have already said, but we repeat them because they are fundamental.

- Make careful to adapt the portion amounts to meet your dog's specific needs. The amount of food required by your dog depends on their breed, size, age, and activity level.
- Before feeding the meat to your dog, remove any bones. Splintered cooked bones can cause internal damage.

- In the recipes, avoid adding any spices or seasonings. Dogs' perception of taste differs from that of humans, and some spices can be toxic to them.
- If you include veggies in the recipes, make sure to properly cook them. Raw veggies can be difficult to digest in dogs and might cause stomach distress.
- Food should be served at room temperature or slightly warm. Hot food should be avoided since it might burn your dog's mouth.
- Begin by giving your dog a tiny quantity of the new food and seeing how they react to it. You can progressively increase the amount of food you offer them if they have no difficulties.

Consult your veterinarian if you are unclear how much food to feed your dog or if you have any other queries regarding their nutrition.

Could you kindly leave a review on Amazon if you like the book and find it helpful? It only takes a few seconds, but it's very important to me. You can do it by scanning the following QR code with your phone. Thank you.

# **MEAT**

# Zucchini and Chicken Bites

**Ingredients**:

- 1/2 cup cooked chicken, shredded
- 1/2 cup zucchini, grated
- 1/4 cup whole wheat flour
- 1 egg
- 1/4 teaspoon baking powder

**Instructions**:

1. Preheat oven to 350 degrees F (175 degrees C).

2. Grease a baking sheet with cooking spray.

3. In a large bowl, combine the chicken, zucchini, flour, egg, and baking powder.

4. Mix well.

5. Form the mixture into small meatballs.

6. Place the meatballs on the prepared baking sheet.

7. Bake for 20-25 minutes, or until the meatballs are cooked through.

8. Let cool completely before serving.

## Ground Beef and Sweet Potato

**Ingredients**:

- 1 pound ground beef
- 1 sweet potato, peeled and diced
- 1/2 cup water

**Instructions**:

1. Brown the ground beef in a large skillet over medium heat.

2. Drain off any excess grease.

3. Add the sweet potato and water to the skillet.

4. Bring to a boil, then reduce heat to low and simmer for 15-20 minutes, or until the sweet potato is tender.

5. Serve immediately.

## Turkey and Vegetable Stew

**Ingredients**:

- 1 pound ground turkey
- 2 carrots, chopped
- 2 celery stalks, chopped

- 1/2 cup green beans, trimmed and cut into 1-inch pieces
- 1/2 cup peas
- 1/2 cup chopped broccoli florets
- 1/2 cup chopped cauliflower florets
- 2 cups beef broth
- 1/2 cup water
- 1/4 teaspoon salt

**Instructions**:

1. Brown the ground turkey in a large pot over medium heat.

2. Drain off any excess grease.

3. Add the carrots, celery, green beans, peas, broccoli, and cauliflower to the pot.

4. Stir to combine.

5. Add the beef broth, water and salt to the pot.

6. Bring to a boil, then reduce heat to low and simmer for 20-25 minutes, or until the vegetables are tender.

7. Serve immediately.

# Lamb and Lentil Soup

**Ingredients**:

- 1 pound ground lamb
- 2 carrots, chopped
- 2 celery stalks, chopped
- 1 cup lentils
- 6 cups beef broth
- 1/4 teaspoon salt

**Instructions**:

1. Brown the ground lamb in a large pot over medium heat.

2. Drain off any excess grease.

3. Add the carrots, celery, and lentils to the pot.

4. Stir to combine.

5. Add the beef broth and salt to the pot.

6. Bring to a boil, then reduce heat to low and simmer for 30-35 minutes, or until the lentils are tender.

7. Serve immediately.

# Beef Meatballs

**Ingredients**:

- 1 pound ground beef
- 1/2 cup bread crumbs

1 egg

**Instructions**:

1. Preheat oven to 400 degrees F (200 degrees C).

2. Line a baking sheet with parchment paper.

3. In a large bowl, combine the ground beef, bread crumbs, egg,

4. Mix well with your hands.

5. Form the mixture into small meatballs.

6. Place the meatballs on the prepared baking sheet.

7. Bake for 15-20 minutes, or until the meatballs are cooked through.

8. Serve immediately.

# Chicken and Liver Pâté

**Ingredients**:

- 1 pound chicken livers
- 1/2 pound butter, softened
- 1/4 cup chopped fresh parsley
- 1/4 teaspoon salt

**Instructions**:

1. In a medium skillet, melt 1/4 cup of the butter over medium heat.

2. Add the chicken livers and cook until browned on all sides.

3. Remove the chicken livers from the skillet and set aside.

Cook until softened.

6. In a food processor, combine the chicken livers, parsley and salt.

7. Process until smooth.

8. Add the remaining 1/2 pound of butter to the food processor and process until combined.

9. Pour the pâté into a serving dish and refrigerate until firm.

10. Serve with crackers or toast.

# Turkey and Cranberry Stuffing

**Ingredients**:

- 1 pound ground turkey
- 1/2 cup bread crumbs
- 1/4 cup chopped celery
- 1/4 cup chopped cranberries
- 1/4 cup chopped fresh parsley
- 1/4 teaspoon salt

**Instructions**:

1. Preheat oven to 375 degrees F (190 degrees C).

2. In a large bowl, combine the ground turkey, bread crumbs, celery, cranberries, parsley and salt.

3. Mix well.

4. Transfer the mixture to a greased baking dish.

5. Bake for 20-25 minutes, or until the turkey is cooked through.

6. Serve immediately.

# Ground Beef and Pumpkin Chili

**Ingredients**:

- 1 pound ground beef
- 1 (15 ounce) can diced tomatoes, undrained
- 1 (15 ounce) can black beans, drained and rinsed
- 1 (15 ounce) can kidney beans, drained and rinsed
- 1 (15 ounce) can pumpkin puree
- 1 (10 ounce) can Rotel tomatoes and green chilies, undrained
- 1/2 teaspoon cumin
- 1/4 teaspoon salt

**Instructions**:

1. Brown the ground beef in a large pot over medium heat.

2. Drain off any excess grease.

Pot and cook until softened.

4. Add the diced tomatoes, black beans, kidney beans, pumpkin puree, Rotel tomatoes and green chilies, chili powder, cumin and salt.

5. Bring to a boil, then reduce heat to low and simmer for 30 minutes, or until the chili has thickened.

6. Serve immediately.

# Chicken and Vegetable Soup

**Ingredients**:

- 1 pound boneless, skinless chicken breasts
- 2 carrots, chopped
- 2 celery stalks, chopped
- 1/2 cup green beans, trimmed and cut into 1-inch pieces
- 1/2 cup peas
- 1/2 cup chopped broccoli florets
- 1/2 cup chopped cauliflower florets
- 8 cups chicken broth

**Instructions**:

1. Place the chicken breasts in a large pot.
2. Add the carrots, celery, green beans, peas, broccoli, and cauliflower to the pot.
3. Add the chicken broth.
4. Bring to a boil, then reduce heat to low and simmer for 30 minutes, or until the chicken is cooked through.
5. Remove the chicken breasts from the pot and shred them.
6. Return the shredded chicken to the pot and serve.

# Beef Stew

**Ingredients**:

- 1 pound beef chuck roast, cut into 1-inch cubes
- 2 carrots, chopped
- 2 celery stalks, chopped
- 1/2 cup green beans, trimmed and cut into 1-inch pieces
- 1/2 cup peas
- 1/2 cup chopped potatoes
- 1/2 cup chopped carrots
- 1/2 cup chopped celery
- 3 cups beef broth

**Instructions**:

1. Preheat oven to 300 degrees F (150 degrees C).
2. Brown the beef cubes in a large skillet over medium heat.
3. Drain off any excess grease.
4. Add the carrots, celery, green beans, peas, potatoes, carrots, celery, beef broth to the skillet.
5. Bring to a boil, then reduce heat to low and cover.
6. Simmer in the preheated oven for 2-3 hours, or until the beef is tender.
7. Serve immediately.

# Chicken Pot Pie

**Ingredients**:

- 1 pound boneless, skinless chicken breasts, cooked and shredded
- 1/2 cup chopped carrots
- 1/2 cup green beans, trimmed and cut into 1-inch pieces
- 1/2 cup peas
- 1/2 cup chopped potatoes
- 1 (10.75 ounce) can cream of chicken soup
- 1/4 cup all-purpose flour
- 1 (9 inch) unbaked pie crust

**Instructions**:

1. Preheat oven to 425 degrees F (220 degrees C).
2. In a large bowl, combine the shredded chicken, carrots, green beans, peas, potatoes, cream of chicken soup, flour.
3. Pour the mixture into the pie crust.
4. Bake in the preheated oven for 30-35 minutes, or until the crust is golden brown and the filling is bubbly.
5. Let cool for 10 minutes before serving.

# Pork and Apple Sauce

**Ingredients**:

- 1 pound boneless, skinless pork chops
- 1/4 cup applesauce
- 1 teaspoon olive oil
- 1/4 teaspoon salt

**Instructions**:

1. Heat the olive oil in a large skillet over medium heat.
2. Season the pork chops with salt.
3. Add the pork chops to the skillet and cook for 3-4 minutes per side, or until cooked through.
4. Remove the pork chops from the skillet and set aside.
5. Add the applesauce to the skillet and cook for 1-2 minutes, or until heated through.
6. Return the pork chops to the skillet and cook for 1-2 minutes more, or until heated through.
7. Serve immediately.

## Chicken and Rice

**Ingredients**:

- 1 cup cooked chicken, shredded
- 1 cup cooked rice
- 1 potato

**Instructions**:

1. 1 sweet potato, peeled and diced
2. 1 cup cooked rice
3. 1/2 cup lactose-free milk
4. Instructions:
5. Steam or boil the sweet potato until tender.
6. Mash the sweet potato with a fork.
7. Add the rice and stir in the milk.
8. Serve immediately.

## Zucchini and Chicken Bites

**Ingredients**:

- 1/2 cup cooked chicken, shredded
- 1/2 cup zucchini, grated
- 1/4 cup whole wheat flour

- 1 egg
- 1/4 teaspoon baking powder

**Instructions**:

1. Preheat oven to 350 degrees F (175 degrees C).
2. Grease a baking sheet with cooking spray.
3. In a large bowl, combine the chicken, zucchini, flour, egg, and baking powder.
4. Mix well.
5. Form the mixture into small meatballs.
6. Place the meatballs on the prepared baking sheet.
7. Bake for 20-25 minutes, or until the meatballs are cooked through.
8. Let cool completely before serving.

## Chicken and Green Bean Soup

**Ingredients**:

- 1 cup cooked chicken, shredded
- 1/2 cup cooked green beans, chopped
- 1/2 cup chicken broth
- 1/4 cup water
- 1 tablespoon mashed potato

**Instructions**:

1. Combine all ingredients in a saucepan.
2. Bring to a boil, then reduce heat and simmer for 10 minutes, or until the soup is heated through.
3. Serve immediately.

## Turkey and Sweet Potato Mash

**Ingredients**:

- 1/2 cup cooked turkey, shredded
- 1/4 cup cooked sweet potato, mashed
- 1/4 cup water
- 1 tablespoon mashed banana
- 1/4 teaspoon parsley, chopped

**Instructions**:

1. Combine all ingredients in a bowl and mix well.
2. Serve immediately.

## Chicken and Quinoa

**Ingredients**:

- 1 cup cooked chicken, shredded
- 1/2 cup cooked quinoa
- 1/4 cup chicken broth
- 1 tablespoon mashed banana
- 1/4 teaspoon parsley, chopped

**Instructions**:

1. Combine all ingredients in a bowl and mix well.
2. Serve immediately.

## Lamb and Lentils

**Ingredients**:

- 1/2 cup cooked lamb, shredded
- 1/4 cup cooked lentils
- 1/4 cup chicken broth
- 1/4 teaspoon dried rosemary

**Instructions**:

1. Combine all ingredients in a bowl and mix well.
2. Serve immediately.

## Turkey and Sweet Potato Mash

**Ingredients**:

- 1/2 cup cooked turkey, shredded
- 1/4 cup cooked sweet potato, mashed
- 1/4 cup water
- 1 tablespoon mashed banana
- 1/4 teaspoon parsley, chopped

**Instructions**: 70

1. Combine all ingredients in a bowl and mix well.
2. Serve immediately.

# **FISH**

## Fish and Sweet Potato

**Ingredients**:

- 1/2 cup cooked fish, flaked
- 1/4 cup cooked sweet potato, mashed
- 1/4 cup chicken broth
- 1/4 teaspoon dried dill

**Instructions**:

1. Combine all ingredients in a bowl and mix well.
2. Serve immediately.

## Salmon and Oatmeal Pancakes

**Ingredients**:

- 1/2 cup cooked salmon, flaked
- 1/4 cup rolled oats
- 1/4 cup water
- 1 egg
- 1/4 teaspoon baking powder

**Instructions:**

1. In a large bowl, combine the salmon, oats, water, egg, and baking powder.
2. Mix well.
3. Heat a small amount of oil in a frying pan over medium heat.
4. Pour a small amount of batter into the pan and cook for 2-3 minutes per side, or until golden brown.
5. Repeat with the remaining batter.
6. Serve immediately.

# Salmon and Quinoa

**Ingredients:**

- 1 salmon fillet, skinless and boneless
- 1 cup quinoa
- 1 cup water
- 1 tablespoon olive oil

**Instructions:**

1. Preheat oven to 400 degrees F (200 degrees C).
2. Place the salmon fillet on a baking sheet lined with parchment paper.
3. Bake for 15-20 minutes, or until the salmon is cooked through.

4. While the salmon is baking, cook the quinoa according to package directions.
5. Once the quinoa is cooked, fluff it with a fork and serve it with the salmon.

## Salmon and Peas

**Ingredients**:

- 1 salmon fillet, skinless and boneless
- 1/2 cup cooked peas

**Instructions**:

1. Flake the salmon fillet with a fork.
2. Mix together the salmon and peas.
3. Serve immediately.

## Tuna and Rice

**Ingredients**:

- 1 can tuna, drained
- 1 cup cooked rice

**Instructions**:

1. Mix together the tuna and rice.
2. Serve immediately.

## Salmon and Oatmeal

**Ingredients**:

- 1 salmon fillet, skinless and boneless
- 1/2 cup cooked oatmeal

**Instructions:**

1. Flake the salmon fillet with a fork.
2. Mix together the salmon and oatmeal.
3. Serve immediately.

## Sardines and Yogurt

**Ingredients**:

- 1 can sardines in spring water, drained
- 1/2 cup plain lactose-free yogurt

**Instructions:**

1. Mash the sardines with a fork.
2. Stir in the yogurt.
3. Serve immediately.

# Fish and Potato

**Ingredients**:

- 1 white fish fillet (such as cod or haddock), skinless and boneless
- 1/2 cup cooked potato, mashed

**Instructions**:

1. Steam or boil the fish fillet until cooked through.
2. Mash the fish with a fork.
3. Stir in the mashed potato.
4. Serve immediately.
5. Frozen Fish and Carrot Pops

## Frozen Fish and Carrot Pops

**Ingredients**:

- 1/2 cup cooked fish, flaked
- 1/2 cup carrot, grated
- 1/4 cup water

**Instructions**:

1. Pour the fish, carrot, and water into ice pop molds.

2. Freeze for 4-6 hours, or until solid and serve.

## Fish and Apple Mash

**Ingredients**:

- 1 white fish fillet (such as cod or haddock), skinless and boneless
- 1/2 apple, peeled and diced
- 1/4 cup water
- 1 tablespoon mashed potato
- 1/4 teaspoon cinnamon

**Instructions**:

1. Steam or boil the fish fillet and apple together until cooked through.
2. Mash the fish and apple with a fork.
3. Stir in the mashed potato and cinnamon.
4. Serve immediately.

## Sardines and Blueberries

**Ingredients**:

- 1 can sardines in spring water, drained
- 1/2 cup lactose-free milk
- 1/4 cup blueberries
- 1/4 cup chopped banana

**Instructions**:

1. Layer the sardines, milk, blueberries, and banana in a glass jar or small bowl.
2. Serve immediately.

## Fish and Vegetable Soup

**Ingredients**:

- 1 white fish fillet (such as cod or haddock), skinless and boneless
- 1/2 cup chopped carrots
- 1/2 cup chopped celery
- 1/2 cup chopped green beans
- 1/4 cup water

**Instructions**:

1. Steam or boil the fish fillet and vegetables together until cooked through.
2. Mash the fish and vegetables with a fork.
3. Stir in the water.
4. Serve immediately.

## Fish and Oat Muffins

**Ingredients**:

- 1 white fish fillet (such as cod or haddock), skinless and boneless, flaked
- 1/2 cup rolled oats
- 1/4 cup water
- 1 egg
- 1/4 teaspoon baking powder

**Instructions**:

1. Preheat oven to 350 degrees F (175 degrees C).
2. Grease a muffin tin with cooking spray.
3. In a large bowl, combine the fish, oats, water, egg, and baking powder.
4. Mix well.
5. Pour the mixture into the prepared muffin tin.

6. Bake for 20-25 minutes, or until a toothpick inserted into the center of a muffin comes out clean. And let cool completely before serving.

## **Fish and Peanut Butter Frosty Paws**

**Ingredients**:

- 1/2 cup cooked fish, flaked
- 1/4 cup peanut butter
- 1/4 cup water
- 1 ripe banana, mashed

**Instructions**:

1. Combine all ingredients in a blender or food processor and blend until smooth.
2. Pour the mixture into ice cube trays or popsicle molds.
3. Freeze for 4-6 hours, or until solid.
4. Serve immediately.

# Tuna and Spinach Treats

**Ingredients**:

- 1 can of tuna in water, drained
- 1 cup fresh spinach

**Instructions**:

1. Blend tuna and spinach together.

2. Form into small balls and refrigerate.

3. Serve as tasty snacks.

# **VEGETABLES**

## Sweet Potato and Carrot Mash

**Ingredients**:

- 1 sweet potato, peeled and diced
- 1 carrot, peeled and diced
- 1/4 cup water
- 1 tablespoon mashed potato
- 1/4 teaspoon parsley, chopped

**Instructions:**

1. Steam or boil the sweet potato and carrot together until cooked through.
2. Mash the sweet potato and carrot with a fork.
3. Stir in the mashed potato, parsley, and water.
4. Serve immediately.

## Pumpkin Pupsicles

**Ingredients**:

- 1/4 cup pumpkin puree
- 1/4 cup water
- 1 tablespoon mashed banana
- 1/4 teaspoon cinnamon

**Instructions:**

1. Combine all ingredients in a blender or food processor and blend until smooth.

2. Pour the mixture into popsicle molds.

3. Freeze for at least 3 hours, or until solid.

4. Serve immediately.


## Pumpkin and Oatmeal Muffins

**Ingredients**:

- 1/2 cup pumpkin puree
- 1/4 cup rolled oats
- 1/4 cup water
- 1 egg
- 1/4 teaspoon baking powder

**Instructions**:

1. Preheat oven to 350 degrees F (175 degrees C).

2. Grease a muffin tin with cooking spray.

3. In a large bowl, combine the pumpkin puree, oats, water, egg, and baking powder.

4. Mix well.

5. Pour the batter into the prepared muffin tin.

6. Bake for 20-25 minutes, or until a toothpick inserted into the center of a muffin comes out clean.

7. Let cool completely before serving.

## Sweet Potato Chews

**Ingredients**:

- 2 sweet potatoes

**Instructions**:

1. Slice sweet potatoes into thin strips.

2. Bake at 250°F (120°C) for 3-4 hours until they become chewy.

3. Cool and serve.

# Carrot Crunchies

**Ingredients**:

- 2 large carrots

**Instructions**:

1. Slice carrots into thin rounds.
2. Bake at 200°F (95°C) for 2-3 hours until they become crunchy.
3. Allow them to cool and give as treats.

# Pumpkin Dog Biscuits

**Ingredients**:

- 2 cups whole wheat flour
- 1/2 cup canned pumpkin
- 2 eggs

**Instructions**:

1. Mix flour, pumpkin, and eggs until a dough forms.
2. Roll out dough and cut into shapes.
3. Bake at 350°F (175°C) for 30 minutes.

# Broccoli Muffins

**Ingredients**:

- 1/2 cup cooked broccoli, chopped
- 1/4 cup whole wheat flour
- 1 egg
- 1/4 teaspoon baking powder

**Instructions**:

1. Preheat oven to 350 degrees F (175 degrees C).
2. Grease a muffin tin with cooking spray.
3. In a large bowl, combine the broccoli, flour, egg, and baking powder.
4. Mix well.
5. Pour the mixture into the prepared muffin tin.
6. Bake for 20-25 minutes, or until a toothpick inserted into the center of a muffin comes out clean.
7. Let cool completely before serving.

# Apple and Carrot Crunchers

**Ingredients**:

- 1 apple, grated
- 1 carrot, grated

**Instructions**:

1. Combine grated apple and carrot.
2. Form into small patties.
3. Dehydrate or bake at 200°F (95°C) until crunchy.

# **EXTRA**

## Peanut Butter and Banana

**Ingredients:**

- 1 tablespoon peanut butter
- 1/2 banana, mashed

**Instructions:**

1. Mix together the peanut butter and banana.
2. Serve immediately.

## Pumpkin and Peanut Butter Ice Cream

**Ingredients:**

- 1/2 cup pumpkin puree
- 1/4 cup peanut butter
- 1/4 cup lactose-free milk
- 1 ripe banana, mashed
- 1/4 teaspoon cinnamon

**Instructions:**

1. Combine all ingredients in a blender or food processor and blend until smooth.

2. Pour the mixture into an ice cream maker and freeze according to the manufacturer's instructions.
3. Serve immediately, or freeze for later.

## Green Bean Smoothie

**Ingredients**:

- 1/2 cup cooked green beans, chopped
- 1/2 cup lactose-free milk
- 1/4 cup banana, mashed
- 1 tablespoon peanut butter
- 1/4 teaspoon pumpkin spice

**Instructions**:

1. Combine all ingredients in a blender or food processor and blend until smooth.
2. Serve immediately.

## Pumpkin and Peanut Butter Ice Cream

**Ingredients**:

- 1/2 cup pumpkin puree
- 1/4 cup peanut butter
- 1/4 cup plain yogurt
- 1 ripe banana, mashed
- 1/4 teaspoon cinnamon

**Instructions**:

1. Combine all ingredients in a blender or food processor and blend until smooth.
2. Pour the mixture into an ice cream maker and freeze according to the manufacturer's instructions.

## Peanut Butter and Banana Dog Cookies

**Ingredients**:

- 1 cup peanut butter (588 calories)
- 1 ripe banana, mashed (105 calories)
- egg (78 calories)
- 1 cup whole wheat flour (345 calories)
- 1/4 cup water (0 calories)

**Instructions:**

1. Preheat oven to 350 degrees F (175 degrees C).
2. Line a baking sheet with parchment paper.
3. In a large bowl, combine the peanut butter, banana, egg, flour, and water.
4. Mix well.
5. Form the dough into small balls.
6. Place the balls on the prepared baking sheet.
7. Bake for 15-20 minutes, or until golden brown. Let cool completely before serving.

## Fruit pudding

**Ingredients**:

- 1/2 cup plain lactose-free milk
- 1/4 cup cooked oatmeal
- 1/4 cup sliced berries

**Instructions**:

1. Layer the yogurt, oatmeal, and berries in a glass jar or small bowl.
2. Serve immediately.
3.

# Carrot Muffins

**Ingredients**:

- 1/4 cup grated carrots (20 calories)
- 1/4 cup whole wheat flour (173 calories)
- 1 egg (78 calories)
- 1/4 teaspoon baking powder (3 calories)

**Instructions**:

1. Preheat oven to 350 degrees F (175 degrees C).

2. Grease a muffin tin with cooking spray.

3. In a large bowl, combine the cottage cheese, carrots, flour, egg, and baking powder.

4. Mix well.

5. Pour the batter into the prepared muffin tin.

6. Bake for 20-25 minutes, or until a toothpick inserted into the center of a muffin comes out clean.

7. Let cool completely before serving.

## Hard-Boiled Egg and Oatmeal

**Ingredients**:

- 1 hard-boiled egg, chopped (78 calories)
- 1/4 cup cooked oatmeal (150 calories)

**Instructions**:

1. Combine the hard-boiled egg and oatmeal in a bowl.
2. Serve immediately.

## Scrambled Egg and Toast

**Ingredients**:

- 1 egg (78 calories)
- 1 slice of whole wheat bread, toasted (165 calories)

**Instructions**:

1. Scramble the egg in a small pan.
2. Toast the bread.
3. Place the scrambled egg on top of the toast.
4. Serve immediately.

## Peanut Butter Kong

**Ingredients**:

- 1 Kong
- 1/4 cup peanut butter (588 calories)

**Instructions**:

1. Fill the Kong with peanut butter.
2. Freeze the Kong for at least 3 hours.
3. Give the Kong to your dog to enjoy.

## Frozen Banana Pops

**Ingredients**:

- 1 ripe banana, peeled and cut into slices (105 calories)
- 1/4 cup lactose-free milk

**Instructions**:

1. Thread the banana slices onto a popsicle stick.
2. Dip the banana slices in milk.

3. Place the popsicle sticks in a freezer-safe container and freeze for at least 3 hours.
4. Serve the frozen banana pops to your dog to enjoy.

## **Apple Muffins**

**Ingredients**:

- 1/2 cup cottage cheese
- 1/4 cup diced apple
- 1/4 cup whole wheat flour
- 1 egg
- 1/4 teaspoon baking powder

1. **Instructions**:
2. Preheat oven to 350 degrees F (175 degrees C).
3. Grease a muffin tin with cooking spray.
4. In a large bowl, combine the cottage cheese, apple, flour, egg, and baking powder.
5. Mix well.
6. Pour the batter into the prepared muffin tin.
7. Bake for 20-25 minutes, or until a toothpick inserted into the center of a muffin comes out clean.
8. Let cool completely before serving.

# Zucchini and Peanut Butter Cookies

**Ingredients**:

- 1/2 cup grated zucchini
- 1/4 cup peanut butter
- 1/4 cup whole wheat flour
- 1 egg
- 1/4 teaspoon baking powder

**Instructions**:

1. Preheat oven to 350 degrees F (175 degrees C).
2. Line a baking sheet with parchment paper.
3. In a large bowl, combine the zucchini, peanut butter, flour, egg, and baking powder.
4. Mix well.
5. Form the dough into small balls.
6. Place the balls on the prepared baking sheet.
7. Bake for 15-20 minutes, or until golden brown.
8. Let cool completely before serving.

## Peanut Butter Frosting

**Ingredients**:

- 1/4 cup peanut butter
- 1 tablespoon water
- 1/4 teaspoon honey

**Instructions**:

1. Combine all ingredients in a blender or food processor and blend until smooth.

2. Serve immediately, or store in the refrigerator for later.

## Peanut Butter Banana Bites

**Ingredients**:

2 ripe bananas

1/2 cup unsalted peanut butter

1/4 cup lactose-free milk

**Instructions**:

1. Mash the bananas and combine with peanut butter and milk.

2. Drop spoonfuls onto a baking sheet and freeze until firm.

3. Serve as a cool treat.

## **Apple Slices**

**Ingredients:**

- 1 apple, sliced

**Instructions**:

1. Remove apple seeds and slice into thin pieces.

2. Serve the slices as a healthy snack.

## **Banana Popsicles**

**Ingredients**:

- 1 ripe banana

**Instructions**:

1. Blend banana.

2. Pour into ice cube trays and freeze.

3. Give your dog a chilled treat.

## Zucchini Bites

**Ingredients**:

- 1 zucchini

**Instructions**:

1. Slice the zucchini into thin rounds.

2. Dehydrate in the oven at 170°F (75°C) for 4-6 hours.

3. Serve as crunchy snacks.

## Banana Oat Biscuits

**Ingredients**:

- 2 ripe bananas
- 1 cup rolled oats

**Instructions**:

1. Mash bananas and mix with oats.
2. Drop spoonfuls onto a baking sheet.
3. Bake at 350°F (175°C) for 10-12 minutes.

# CONCLUSION

As we conclude our tour through the realm of canine nutrition and provide some simple, healthful meals for your furry companion, it's essential to focus on the significance of feeding your dog a balanced and nutritious diet. Your dog is more than a pet; they are a beloved member of your family, and their well-being is critical.

We've covered many elements of canine nutrition in this book, from understanding their nutritional needs to producing tasty homemade meals that meet their dietary demands. We've learned about the key elements that their bodies require, the importance of protein, carbs, fats, vitamins, and minerals, and how to make informed decisions when purchasing commercial dog food.

We've also discussed the advantages of creating homemade meals for your dog, such as having more control over the materials, avoiding hazardous chemicals, and adapting to your dog's individual requirements and tastes. We've included a variety of simple recipes that can be prepared quickly and with few ingredients, ensuring that your dog gets nutritional and tasty meals.

However, keep in mind that, while the recipes in this book are intended to promote health and well-being, they should be seen as supplements to your dog's overall diet. Before making substantial changes to your dog's nutrition, always speak with a trained veterinarian, especially if they have underlying health concerns, allergies, or unique dietary demands.

We have a responsibility as responsible pet owners to provide our dogs with the best possible care, which includes providing them with appropriate nourishment. Proper nutrition is the cornerstone of good health, and it is critical to your dog's vigor, energy, and longevity.

The following are some major insights from this book:

Recognizing Your Dog's Nutritional demands: Dogs have distinct nutritional demands, and recognizing these needs is the first step toward providing a balanced diet for them.

While many commercial dog feeds are created to fulfill nutritional criteria, cooking homemade meals allows you to have more control over the ingredients and provides more variety.

Fresh items Have Power: Including fresh items in your dog's meal might improve their general health. Fresh fruits and vegetables, as well as lean meats, can be beneficial additions to their diets.

Diet Modification: Because each dog is unique, their dietary requirements may differ. Whether your dog is a high-energy working dog or a geriatric pet, their food must be tailored to their needs.

Balanced Recipes: The recipes in this book are balanced to fulfill the nutritional needs of your dog. However, it is essential to adhere to portion sizes and check your dog's weight in order to maintain a good physical condition.

Consultation with Your Veterinarian: A veterinarian is your best bet for tailored nutritional recommendations. For your dog's long-term health, regular check-ups and conversations about his nutrition are vital.

Finally, the goal of this book has been to give you with knowledge and practical recipes to help you provide a better and happier life for your dog. You are making a huge investment in your dog's well-being by taking the time to study their specific nutritional needs and including prepared meals into their diet. Remember that your relationship with your dog extends beyond meals. Your love, care, and company are equally important to their happiness. So, keep nourishing their body and spirit, and treasure the moments you enjoy with your devoted partner.

Here's to a future filled with happy fetch sessions, wagging tails, and the contented satisfaction of knowing you're giving your dog the best.

Thank you for joining us on this exploration of canine nutrition. I wish you and your pet many happy and healthy years together!

Hey! 🐾 Just finished "Homemade Healthy Dog Food"? If it got those tails wagging and you enjoyed the recipes, spill the beans! I'm all ears (and paws)! 📖🐶

Please, leave a review on Amazon by framing the following QR code with your mobile phone camera.

### Thank you!

# JASMINE FOSTER

Jasmine Foster, a passionate 42-year-old American journalist and author, has dedicated her career to advocating for animals through her writing. With a deep love for dogs, Jasmine's work transcends the boundaries of traditional journalism as she delves into the world of our four-legged friends. Her insightful articles and heartwarming stories capture the essence of the human-animal bond, emphasizing the importance of compassion and responsible pet care. As both a seasoned journalist and an accomplished author, Jasmine Foster's commitment to shedding light on the joys and challenges of life with dogs resonates with readers, fostering a deeper understanding of the unique and enriching relationships we share with our canine companions. Through her words, she not only informs but also inspires, creating a lasting impact in the hearts of those who share her love for our furry friends.

# BONUS 1

## 7 MISTAKES YOU MIGHT BE MAKING WITH YOUR DOG'S NUTRITION

Nutrition is the cornerstone of your dog's health and happiness. The choices you make regarding their diet can significantly impact their overall well-being. In this chapter, we'll delve into seven common mistakes that dog owners frequently make without realizing it, and we'll explore how to avoid these pitfalls to ensure that your furry companion enjoys a long and healthy life.

## Mistake 1: Overfeeding

Overfeeding is a mistake that many well-intentioned dog owners unknowingly make. It's easy to spoil your furry friend with extra treats or larger portions, but this can lead to obesity, a problem that affects a significant number of dogs. Obesity, in turn, can lead to a host of health issues, including diabetes, heart disease, joint problems, and a shorter lifespan.

To prevent overfeeding, it's essential to follow the recommended feeding guidelines provided by your dog's food manufacturer. These guidelines take into account your dog's age, size, activity level, and other factors. Additionally, consult with your veterinarian to determine the ideal portion size for your dog.

## Mistake 2: Feeding a One-Size-Fits-All Diet

Just as every person's dietary needs vary, so do those of dogs. Feeding a generic, one-size-fits-all diet may not provide your dog with the specific nutrients they require. Various factors, including breed, age, activity level, and any underlying health issues, influence what's best for your pet.

Consider, for instance, the dietary needs of a large, active breed like a Labrador Retriever compared to a small, less active breed like a Shih Tzu. Their nutritional requirements differ significantly. Puppies, adults, and senior dogs also have distinct needs, and these must be considered when selecting the right food for your dog. Consulting a veterinarian or a canine nutritionist can be incredibly helpful in determining a diet that's tailored to your dog's individual requirements.

## Mistake 3: Ignoring Ingredient Labels

One common oversight when choosing dog food is not paying enough attention to the ingredient labels. It's important to read the labels carefully to understand precisely what your dog is consuming. Look for high-quality protein sources such as chicken, turkey, or salmon. Whole grains like brown rice, oats, or quinoa can provide essential nutrients and fiber. In contrast, foods with excessive fillers, such as corn or wheat, should be avoided.

Moreover, artificial additives, colors, and preservatives offer little to no nutritional value and can sometimes be detrimental. Select a dog food that prioritizes real, natural ingredients and avoids unnecessary additives for your pet's overall health and well-being.

## Mistake 4: Inconsistent Feeding Schedule

Dogs thrive on routine. An inconsistent feeding schedule can disrupt their digestive system and metabolism, leading to discomfort and digestive issues. To maintain your dog's health, stick to a consistent feeding schedule. Most dogs benefit from being fed at the same times each day. This practice helps them know when to expect their meals and regulates their digestion.

However, the specific schedule can vary depending on your dog's age, daily routine, and individual needs. If you're unsure about the right mealtime frequency and timing for your dog, consult your veterinarian for guidance.

## Mistake 5: Feeding Human Food

The desire to share your food with your dog is understandable, but not all human foods are safe for them. Some common foods are toxic to dogs, including chocolate, grapes, onions, and items containing artificial sweeteners like xylitol. High-fat and spicy foods can upset their stomach and lead to digestive problems or more severe health issues.

It's best to stick to dog-specific treats and foods that are safe and healthy for your pet. If you're ever in doubt about whether a particular human food is safe for your dog, consult your veterinarian for advice.

## Mistake 6: Inadequate Hydration

Water is a fundamental component of your dog's overall health. Dehydration can result in various health problems and discomfort. It's essential to ensure that your dog has access to clean, fresh water at all times. Regularly check their water bowl to guarantee that it is clean and full.

In hot weather or after physical activity, your dog may need more water to stay properly hydrated. Be mindful of their water intake, and provide additional water as necessary. Dehydration can lead to issues such as urinary tract problems and heatstroke, so it's crucial to make hydration a priority.

## Mistake 7: Neglecting Dental Health

While nutrition pertains to what your dog eats, oral health is a vital yet often overlooked aspect of their overall well-being. Neglecting your dog's dental hygiene can lead to dental problems, including tartar buildup, gum disease, and tooth decay. These issues can not only be painful but also contribute to systemic health problems.

To maintain your dog's dental health, incorporate dental care into their routine. Regularly brushing your dog's teeth with dog-specific toothpaste and a soft brush can help prevent plaque and tartar buildup. Additionally, consider providing dental chews, toys, or treats designed to promote oral health. Your veterinarian can also perform dental check-ups as part of your dog's routine healthcare.

In conclusion, providing your dog with proper nutrition is a fundamental aspect of responsible pet ownership. These seven common mistakes, while easy to make, can have significant repercussions on your dog's health and happiness. By avoiding these pitfalls and taking your dog's unique needs into account, you can help ensure that your four-legged companion enjoys a long and vibrant life. Remember that when you have questions or concerns about your dog's diet and nutrition, consulting with your veterinarian or a qualified canine nutritionist is always a wise choice to ensure your dog's dietary needs are met comprehensively.

# BONUS 2

# UNLEASHING THE MAGIC OF DOG TRAINING

Hey there, fellow dog lovers! Welcome to Chapter 4 of our dog training journey. In this chapter, we're going to dive deep into the world of dog training, sharing tips, tricks, and insights to help you become the ultimate dog whisperer.

The Basics of Dog Training: A Quick Recap

Before we start exploring the nitty-gritty details, let's quickly recap the basics. Dog training is all about building a strong, loving, and respectful bond with your furry friend. It's not just about teaching them commands; it's about understanding their needs and communicating effectively.

1. Positive Reinforcement: Remember, positive reinforcement is your secret weapon. Praise, treats, and affection work wonders in motivating your pup. When they do something good, make sure they know it!

2. Consistency is Key: Dogs thrive on routine. Whether it's potty training or leash walking, consistency is your best friend. Set clear rules and stick to them.

3. Patience, Patience, Patience: Your dog is not a furry Einstein. They won't get it the first time, and that's okay. Be patient, and keep repeating the training until they nail it.

4. Socialization: Get your pup out there to meet other dogs and people. Socialization is crucial for a well-adjusted, happy dog.

Now, let's get into the nitty-gritty!

Leash Training: Walk the Walk

Leash training can be a real pain in the behind, but it's a necessary evil. Start by getting your dog comfortable with the leash. Let them wear it around the house and reward them for not turning it into a chew toy.

When you're ready to venture outside, keep the leash short and let your pup know you're the pack leader. If they pull, stop and wait until they slacken the leash. Praise and reward them for walking nicely.

Potty Training: No More Accidents

Potty training can test your patience, but with a little know-how, you can minimize accidents.

1. Frequent Breaks: Take your pup out frequently, especially after meals and playtime.

2. Crate Training: Dogs are naturally clean animals. A crate can be a useful tool in potty training. Just make sure it's a cozy and inviting space, not a prison.

3. Accidents Happen: When they do, don't lose your cool. Clean up the mess with an enzymatic cleaner to remove any lingering scents that might encourage a repeat performance.

Basic Commands: Sit, Stay, and More

Teaching commands is where the real fun begins. Start with basic commands like 'sit,' 'stay,' and 'come.' Here's how:

1. Sit: Hold a treat above your dog's head and move it backward. Most dogs will naturally sit to follow the treat.

2. Stay: Start with 'sit.' Once they're sitting, show your open palm and say 'stay.' Gradually increase the time they need to stay seated before rewarding them.

3. Come: Get down to their level, open your arms, and call them enthusiastically. Reward them when they come to you.

## Advanced Training: Tricks and Agility

If you've mastered the basics, it's time to up the ante. Teach your dog fun tricks like 'roll over,' 'play dead,' or 'high-five.' These tricks not only impress your friends but also stimulate your dog's mind.

Agility training is another exciting way to keep your pup in shape and mentally engaged. Set up a mini obstacle course in your backyard or a nearby park and guide your dog through jumps, tunnels, and weave poles.

## Dealing with Behavioral Issues

No dog is perfect, and behavioral issues may arise. Whether it's barking, digging, or chewing, it's essential to address these problems promptly.

1. Barking: Determine the cause of the barking. Is it boredom, fear, or excitement? Address the root issue, and use commands like 'quiet' or 'enough' to stop excessive barking.

2. Digging: Dogs often dig out of boredom. Provide them with a designated digging area, like a sandbox, and reward them for using it.

3. Chewing: Provide plenty of chew toys and redirect your dog's attention when they start chewing something they shouldn't.

The Bottom Line: Love, Respect, and Fun

In the end, dog training is about more than just commands and tricks. It's about building a loving and respectful relationship with your furry companion. Make training fun, filled with praise and affection, and you'll have a loyal and well-behaved dog by your side in no time.

Remember, every dog is unique, so adapt your training methods to suit their personality and needs. Stay patient, and keep the treats handy. With time and effort, you'll become the ultimate dog trainer and your pup's very best friend. Happy training!

# BONUS 3

# LET'S HAVE FUN TOGETHER!

The following games strengthen your bond with the dog and stimulate them mentally. Have fun!

1. Playing "Hide and Seek":

- Begin by giving your dog one of his or her favorite toys or treats.

Allow your dog to watch while you conceal the object in a spot that is not too difficult to find either inside the home or outside.

After you have concealed the object, encourage your dog to look for it by giving him orders such as "find" and "search."

When your dog locates the object, congratulate them and give them a reward in the form of a tasty bite-sized snack or treat.

2. "Food Puzzle":

- Go out and get a toy like a Kong or one that is very similar to it that has a secret compartment meant to hold food or treats.

- Dog food or treats should be placed within it.

Allow your dog to play with the toy so that it may get the food inside. They will need to put in physical labor in order to obtain the food, which will be psychologically stimulating.

3. Tips and Commands:

Choose commands or tricks that your dog is not familiar with yet so that you may teach them to him.

- When your dog successfully completes the command or trick, you should use some type of positive reinforcement, such as cookies or praise.

- Teach your dog the fundamental instructions such as "sit" and "down" before moving on to more sophisticated maneuvers such as "roll over" and "spin."

4. Games That Stimulate Mental Activation:

Purchase some interactive puzzles or brain stimulation activities that are developed just for canines.

- Stuff them with food or treats, and then watch as your dog tries to figure out how to acquire the goodies by solving the problem.

These games may be as easy or as tough as you want them to be, so begin with the simpler ones and work your way up to the more challenging ones.

5. Play the "Command Retrieval Game" to win:

- You should teach your dog the command for retrieving, such as "fetch" or "bring."

Use a toy or object that your dog is able to pick up and carry in their mouth without any difficulty.

You should toss the item for your dog to find, and after they do, you should give them the instruction to bring it back to you.

- It is important that you praise and thank your dog when they have successfully brought back the item.

The most important thing is to ensure that your dog has fun while playing the activities, and to do so in a secure setting. Adjust the difficulty of the games based on the capabilities of your pet, and be sure to constantly offer positive reinforcement in order to foster the desired behavior.

Printed in Great Britain
by Amazon